MW01538152

Bible Verse Coloring Book

Bible Verse Coloring Book

©2019 – All rights reserved.

No part of this book may be reproduced in whole or in part without the express permission of the publisher

Classic Christian Publishers – Knoxville, TN.

AND WE KNOW

THAT ALL THINGS

Work Together
For Good

To Them That
Love God

To Them Who are
The Called

ACCORDING TO

HIS PURPOSE

Romans 8:28

Psalm 46:1

GOD
is our
Refuge and Strength
A VERY PRESENT HELP IN
Trouble

In the beginning

God

created the

heaven

and the

earth

Genesis 1:1

Trust in the
Lord
with all thine heart;
and lean not unto
thine own
understanding

Proverbs 3:5

In all thy ways
ACKNOWLEDGE
Him
and he shall direct
thy paths

Proverbs 3:6

For by grace are ye saved through *faith* and that not of yourselves: it is the gift of *God*

Ephesians 2:8

I am crucified with Christ: nevertheless I live; yet not I, but Christ liveth in ME

Galatians 2:20

If we confess our sins, he is *faithful* and just to forgive us our sins, and to cleanse us from all unrighteousness

1 John 1:9

But God commendeth his love toward us, in that, while we were yet sinners, Christ died for us

Romans 5:8

But HE was wounded for our transgressions, he was bruised for our iniquities: the chastisement of our peace was upon him; and with his stripes we are healed

ISAIAH 53:5

All scripture is given by

INSPIRATION

OF

God

AND IS

profitable for doctrine,

for reproof,

for correction

FOR INSTRUCTION

in righteousness

II TIMOTHY 3:16

But seek ye first
the kingdom of
God,
and his righteousness;
and all these things
shall be added
unto you

Matthew 6:33

1 PETER 5:7

CASTING ALL YOUR CARE UPON

HIM

FOR HE CARETH
FOR YOU

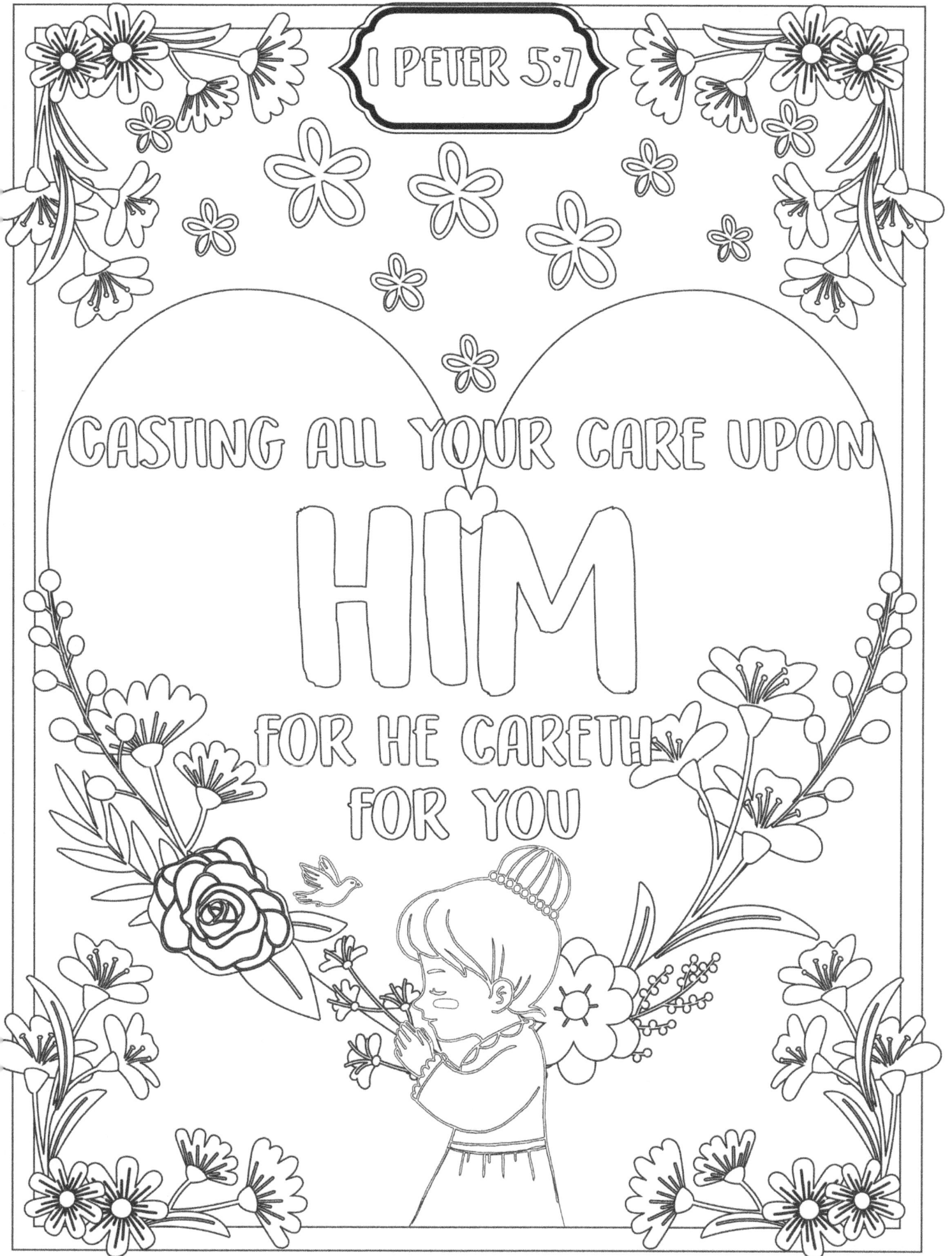

Come unto me, all ye that LABOUR and are heavy laden, and I will give you REST

Matthew 11:28

Therefore if any man be in **Christ** he is a new creature: old things are passed away; behold, all things are become **New**

II Corinthians 5:17

For whosoever shall call upon the name of the Lord shall be saved

Romans 10:13

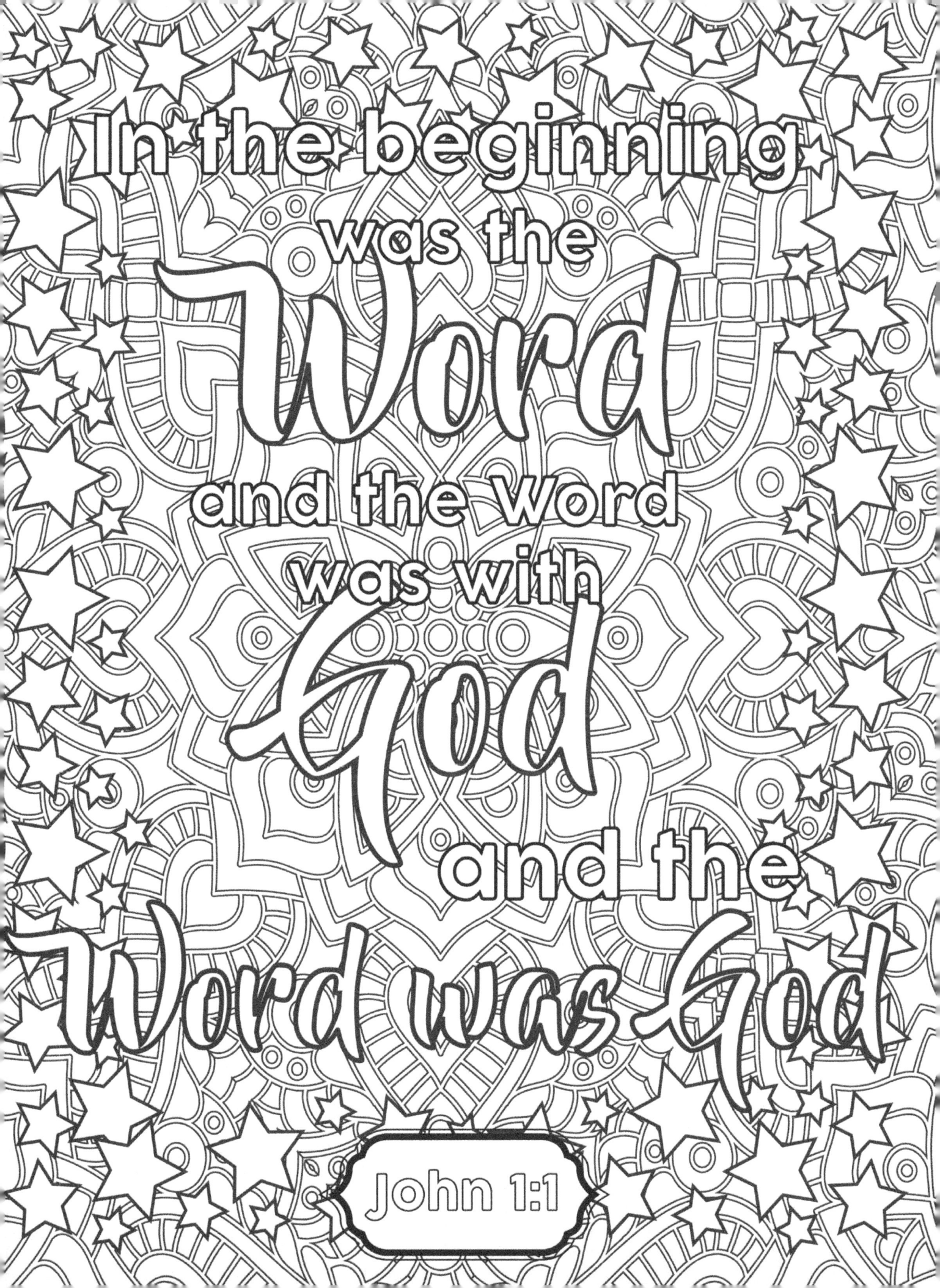

In the beginning was the **Word** and the Word was with **God** and the **Word was God**

John 1:1

And the peace of **God,** which passeth all understanding, shall keep your hearts and minds through **Christ Jesus**

Philippians 4:7

I AM THE WAY, THE TRUTH, AND THE LIFE: NO MAN COMETH UNTO THE FATHER, BUT BY ME

John 14:6

The
LORD
is my
Shepherd
I SHALL NOT
WANT
Psalm 23:1

Psalm 23:2

He maketh me
TO LIE DOWN
in
Green Pastures
He leadeth me
BESIDE THE STILL
waters

HE
RESTORETH
MY SOUL:
He Leadeth Me
IN THE PATHS
OF
Righteousness
FOR
HIS NAME'S
SAKE

PSALM 23:3

Yea,
Though I Walk
Through the Valley
of the
SHADOW OF DEATH,
I will Fear
No Evil

Psalm 23:4a

For Thou Art
With Me;
Thy Rod
AND
Thy Staff
They Comfort Me
Psalm 24:4b

Thou Preparest

A Table

Before Me

in the presence

of mine enemies

PSALM 23:5A

Thou Anointest

MY HEAD WITH OIL

My Cup

RUNNETH

Over

Psalm 23:5b

SURELY GOODNESS AND MERCY shall follow me ALL THE DAYS OF MY LIFE

Psalm 23:6a

What shall we then say
to these things?

If God be for us,

Who can be against us?

Romans 8:31

AND
I will Dwell
IN THE HOUSE
of the
Lord
FOREVER
Psalm 23:6b

I can do all
things through
Christ
which
strengtheneth
me

Philippians 4:13

Be careful for nothing;
but in every thing
by prayer
and supplication
with thanksgiving let
your requests be made
known unto

God

Philippians 4:6

And the life which I now live in the flesh I live by the faith of the Son of God, who loved me, and gave himself for me

Galatians 2:20b

"And be ye kind one to another, Tenderhearted forgiving one another, Even As God for Christ's sake Hath Forgiven You."

EPHESIANS 4:32

"And he saith unto them, Follow me, and I will make you fishers of men."

MATTHEW 4:19

Sing UNTO THE LORD, BLESS HIS NAME; SHEW FORTH HIS SALVATION FROM DAY TO DAY "

PSALMS 96:2

"Thou wilt keep him in perfect peace, whose mind is stayed on thee: because he trusteth in thee."

ISAIAH 26:3

"FOR THE WAGES of sin is death; but the gift of God IS ETERNAL LIFE Through JESUS CHRIST OUR LORD."

Romans 6:23

"For to me TO LIVE IS CHRIST, and to die is Gain"

Philippians 1:21

"Let your light SO SHINE Before Men, THAT THEY MAY SEE Your Good Works, AND GLORIFY YOUR FATHER Which is in Heaven."

MATTHEW 5:16

"NOW FAITH is the SUBSTANCE of things HOPED FOR, the evidence of things NOT SEEN."

HEBREWS 11:1

"BUT SEEK YE FIRST the kingdom of God AND HIS RIGHTEOUSNESS; And all these things Shall be added Unto you. "

MATTHEW 6:33

THY WORD HAVE I HID IN MINE HEART THAT I MIGHT NOT SIN AGAINST THEE

PSALMS 119:11

The End

Thank you for purchasing. Look for more coloring books from us in the future

- Classic Christian Publishers – Knoxville, TN

Made in the USA
Las Vegas, NV
29 January 2022

42599867R00050